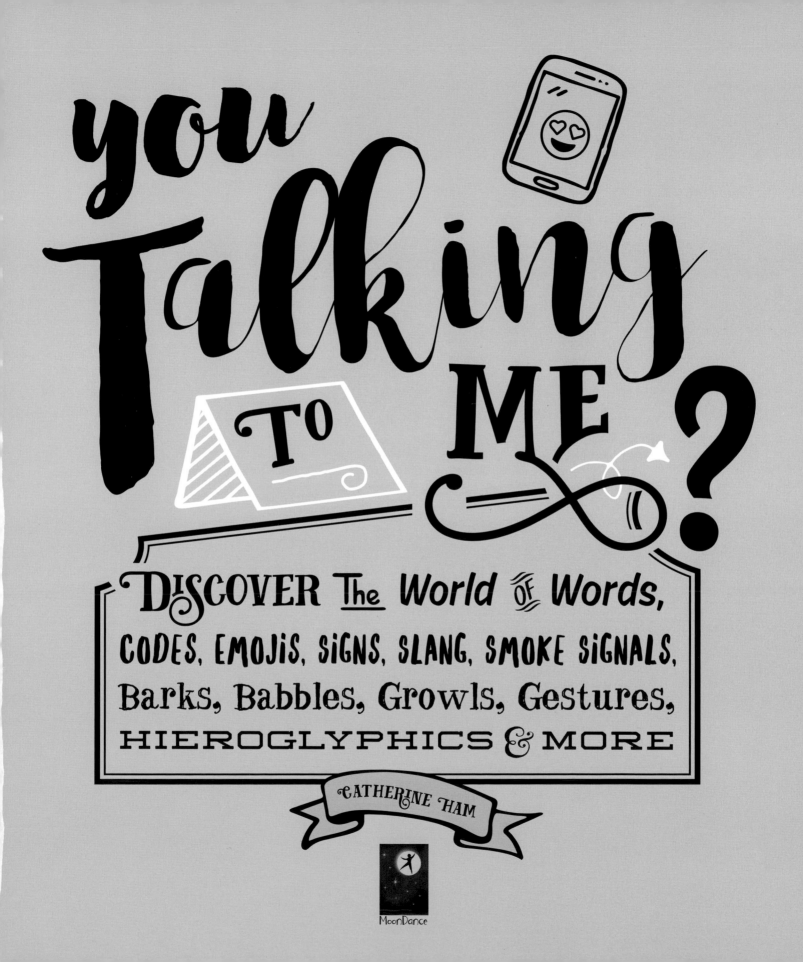

Quarto is the authority on a wide range of topics.
Quarto educates, entertains, and enriches the lives of our readers—
enthusiasts and lovers of hands-on living.
www.quartoknows.com

Design and Layout: Melissa Gerber
Editing: Dawn Cusick
Proofreading: Meredith Hale

{ To cousin Diane, who loves language as I do }

MoonDance

6 Orchard Road, Suite 100
Lake Forest, CA 92630
quartoknows.com
Visit our blogs at quartoknows.com

Printed in China
1 3 5 7 9 10 8 6 4 2

Contents

こんにちは

Introduction

Growing up, I was fortunate to hear lots of languages spoken. Greek, Italian, French, Dutch, German, Afrikaans, Hungarian, Zulu, Polish, Russian, Armenian, and more — I loved listening to people speaking in so many different sounds, and hearing all those new and exciting words. What were they saying? I would try to figure it out by watching their hands and faces, and their body movements. The way we use language, the way we speak, tells others who we are.

Words are so much more than communication, however. They can entertain us in endless ways through games and puzzles. Think for a moment about the words *orange* and *silver*. These are the names of two colors, and also the names of a fruit and a mineral. But did you know that neither of these words has a word that really rhymes with it, even though the English language contains well over a million words? There are a few other words with no rhymes that you can look up if you want to.

You are reading this because you know how to, and you are able to write, right? But spoken and written words are only a part of how we humans are able to talk to each other. Today, we can hold conversations from continent to continent, and send messages in many ways. There's no end to how we can communicate, with and without speaking. We live in a most modern time, but ancient peoples didn't do too badly when it came to passing along important news.

Animals don't speak, of course, but they do use sounds, chemicals, colors, and movements to communicate. Elephants can be heard for miles, though they are not the loudest of creatures, and it's now known that even ants make sounds. The many ways animals get their messages across may boggle your mind!

I also have a message, and I'm sending it to you: I hope very much that you will love language as much as I do.

Cathy Ham

Reaching for Speech

Only humans can *speak*. We know that animals *communicate*. They use calls to pass on information, but they cannot express thoughts and ideas as we do. Their *replies* are very limited. Can animals really have a conversation? Humans can!

SPEECH

Speech uses the sounds we make through our voices to form words. We use speech to tell others what we think. We understand each other because we use words that people in our group know. We repeat these words in ways that make sense. Whether spoken or written, the words have a pattern. This is what we call *language*.

BRAINY

Many animals have bigger brains than ours, but only humans have special language centers to process speech. Without a healthy brain, humans cannot learn to speak. Accidents or illnesses can rob people of their speech. (Check out chapter 3 to learn more about the ways animals communicate.)

PLAYING THEIR PART

To speak, we use a voice box called the *larynx*, which isn't an easy word to say. Vocal cords in the larynx control what our voice sounds like, and how loudly we can speak. The shape of the mouth matters in producing sound.

SPEAKING PARTS

Our tongue moves as we form words. Without a tongue, we could only make noises. Our lips and teeth play a part, too, together with our jaw, in forming words. When speakers have missing teeth, the tongue can get caught up in the empty spaces, making them difficult to understand.

SPIT IT OUT!

You probably never thought much about saliva, did you? It's very hard to speak clearly if your mouth is dry. Your mouth can go dry when you are nervous, or when you're sick. There are also health conditions where people make too much saliva, which can make it hard to speak.

CAN YOU HEAR ME?

We need to hear well to be able to copy and process language sounds. Children who are born deaf or who lose their hearing very early cannot learn to talk without help from speech therapists.

WHO KNEW?

As we form words, our breathing must be under control. Have you ever tried to talk to someone after you've been running? Or *while* you're running? Throat problems can affect speech, too. Remember how you sound with a sore throat?

Finding Our Voices

When did humans start *speaking*? Language experts, called *linguists*, are not sure, but it was certainly a very long time ago. We must have made *sounds*. We would have used our *hands* and *heads* to nod and point the way to food. But how much information can you pass on that way?

CAN'T SEE YOU

At some point, gestures and grunts were no longer enough. We couldn't see hands and heads in the dark. Even by day, our hands were busy finding food and carrying out different tasks. We couldn't always see every person in the group, which needed to stay together to survive.

QUICKLY

Our lives would have depended on quick communication. You don't stand around making hand signals if something's about to eat you! We had to develop a better way to pass on information. It's quicker and easier to do this by voice.

WHAT?

The sounds we made were repeated. They started to mean the same thing to everyone in the group. We kept adding words, with new and different meanings. People could understand what was being said, and could reply. We had begun to create language.

WHO WAS FIRST?

We will never know what the very first language was.
There must have been many early languages, but fossils don't record voice. What did our earliest ancestors sound like? If we heard these sounds today, we would not understand them!

BETTER & BETTER

Humans are very creative. We never stop inventing and improving things. We are full of ideas. Once we started speaking, there was no stopping us.

People began making new words. Some of these words stayed in the language being formed, while others would have vanished. We were already choosing the words we needed.

MORE!

As humans became better at making ourselves understood, we were learning how to put words together in meaningful ways. We call these word combinations *sentences*. Being able to communicate meant that we could pass on useful information.

Over & Over Again

We learn by *repeating*. We say or do something in a certain way, until we know it well. Our speaking improved as we began to learn *voice control* and many new words. Slowly, very slowly, we built a standard way of how we should speak. These *rules* of a language are known as its *grammar*.

YES, BUT . . .

Do you have to use proper grammar to make yourself understood? What if someone's trying to speak a foreign language? Maybe that person's grammar is not the best, but you will still understand if he or she asks: "Please, the train station, where is?"

NO EXCUSES

Foreigners are to be admired for learning a new language, and their mistakes are part of the learning process. We should make every effort to speak our own language correctly, though. Whether it's right to do so or not, people often judge you by the way you speak.

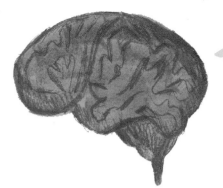

BRAIN GAIN

Our brain collects and stores information in what we call *memory*. Thanks to our memory we can learn and remember new words, and use them again and again as we develop our language skills. The more we learn, the more our brains develop.

BABBLE, BABBLE

Think about a baby learning to speak. Even very young infants make all kinds of noises, quite apart from crying. They watch our faces as we talk to them, and soon start making noises back at us. We usually call this *babbling*. Is babbling a language, though? Should sounds be called a language if nobody else can understand them?

MAMA!

We know from the work of language experts that babies make very similar babbling noises, no matter what language their parents or caregivers speak.

From these basic sounds — and copying what they hear — babies gradually learn to talk in their family's language. This is called the *mother tongue*, or native language. This is our first language.

Big Word Alert!

Do you know any *polyglots*? Who? What? A polyglot is a person who speaks more than one language. The word comes to us from the Greek language, and means "many tongued."

IT'S OFFICIAL

Canada is an example of a country with more than one official language. English and French are the two languages most spoken by Canadians, and those who can speak both are called *bilingual*. Canadian immigrants speak several other languages. Canada's native peoples speak at least sixty-five different languages. What a treasure trove of languages!

NOT UNUSUAL

Some other countries are officially bilingual, too, such as Cyprus, Finland, and Ireland, to mention a few. What other examples of officially bilingual countries can you find? What about countries with even more than two official languages? Belgium uses Dutch, French, and German, while Switzerland uses French, German, and Italian.

DOING AS THE ROMANS DID

Romansh, a language spoken in a certain area of Switzerland, is a fourth official Swiss language. It developed from the Latin spoken at the time of the Roman Empire, and is used today by fewer than one hundred thousand native speakers. There are several dialects, though some are rapidly dying out.

IMPRESSIVE!

South Africa has eleven official languages. The language groups are spread around different areas of the country, but English and Afrikaans are the languages used by the government. Many South Africans can speak several languages. English is the fourth most spoken first language, while Zulu has the largest number of people who speak it as their first language.

COUNTING THEM

No polyglot will ever be able to speak all of the seven thousand languages still spoken in the world. How many languages can you name? How many languages do you hear spoken in your family, your school, and your neighborhood?

Do you speak English?

If so, you share that language with about **1.5 billion** other people. English is the first language of sixty-seven nations, but it's spoken as a **second language** almost all over the world. English is a very important language, but **Chinese** is the language spoken by the biggest group of people in the world. Spanish, English, and Hindi are next on the list.

DO YOU KNOW WHAT YOU KNOW?

You may say that you speak only one language. But actually, your language is full of words from other languages. Did you know that more than 60 percent of English has its beginnings, or roots, in Greek and Latin? English also has many words from German, French, Dutch, Arabic, and several other languages.

YOU DIDN'T KNOW, DID YOU?

Did you know that *jungle* is a word we borrowed from India? We took the word *zero* from Arabic, and the word *million* from Old French, which nicked it from Italian. British traders brought *ketchup* from the Malayan language, which got it from the Chinese. The Spanish probably introduced the banana from West Africa to the English, or maybe it was the Portuguese. But you don't have to go bananas working this all out — linguists do it for us!

ROOTS & TREES

Linguists group languages into about 140 families. Each language family has common roots from which it grew. These roots come from different parts of the world, such as Africa, Europe, and Asia. From these roots, which we call *proto-languages*, all languages developed.

FIRST & FOREMOST

Greek has been spoken for at least five thousand years, and is the oldest living language on record. The word *proto* means *first* in Greek. Ancient Greek writings have enormous importance in the world, from literature and history to all branches of science.

THEN & NOW

Greek was widely used in the ancient world. Language changes, and Greek is no exception. It has been through several periods of development, from proto-Greek to modern Greek.

Let's Borrow That

Language is *alive*. It grows and grows, constantly borrowing words from other languages. Foreign words are taken into a *language* if speakers find them useful. We often need *new words* for things in our quickly changing world. These become part of the language as more people use them.

NEW WORDS

Words have made their way into other languages for centuries. Merchants and adventurers traveled the world, meeting new cultures and learning new languages. They not only brought back goods, new ideas, and wonderful stories, but also a great many different foreign words. Do you know much about ancient explorers and their incredible journeys?

A BOOK OF WORDS

Do you have a dictionary? You know what that is, right? All the words of a particular language are arranged together in alphabetical order. Dictionaries also contain meanings, spellings, and pronunciations.

Some dictionaries contain two languages in one book. When students are learning a new language, they may spend a lot of time with their bilingual dictionary.

WORDS ABOUT WORDS

Many dictionaries include other information, as well. They explain the origin of words and give their plural forms. They may show that a word is *obsolete*, meaning that it's no longer in use.

Words new to the language are called *neologisms*, from the Greek words for new (*neo*) and word (*logos*). You can learn a lot from a dictionary.

PAPER OR SCREEN?

The more information there is in a dictionary, the bigger it will be. The bigger it is and the more pages it has, the heavier it is. "Actually, no," you might say, "I use an online dictionary. It weighs nothing and takes up no space on my bookshelf." A hundred years ago, an online dictionary would have meant nothing to an English speaker. He or she might have thought *online* meant the book was on a line.

LINING UP NEW WORDS

The words *on* and *line* have now come to be used in another way. The ways we can put these two words together have increased, so our language has developed a little bit more. It has grown to meet our needs.

Keeping Track of Our Words

Let's say you were talking to your friend. Can you *remember* exactly what you said? Have you ever had an *argument* with someone about who said what? Unless spoken words are captured in some way, they are *gone forever*, lost as soon as we've said them. No one has a memory good enough to remember, exactly, every single word he or she has ever *said* or *heard*.

SAVING VOICES

We have many ways to record sound nowadays. Can you think of some? What about voice mail? Much of what we watch on TV, for example, has been recorded. This means it can be played over and over again, and the picture and sound are always the same.

ON AIR!

A live television broadcast is a little different, as there is no way to correct a mistake immediately. If it's a bad mistake, it will be edited out before that piece is shown again, but then it's a recording and no longer a live broadcast.

MAKING PROGRESS

The technology used to record voices and sound improves all the time. Recordings from several years ago often don't work on modern equipment, and may be lost unless they are re-recorded on new systems. With advances in technology, the quality of older sound recordings can usually be greatly improved. We can truly hear words and voices from the past.

TELLING TALES, SINGING SONGS

Storytellers and singers of songs have passed words down orally from generation to generation. These words may have been "saved" for quite a long while, but even then the words get changed as the centuries go by.

PUT IT IN WRITING

When you want to remember something, do you write it down? Writing is a way to record thoughts and words. You may want to keep these words for only a short time, like when you write a to-do list. Until you throw it away, the words on that list remain. You can read them again and again.

✓ TO-DO LIST

- Thank-you note to Granny & Grandpa
- Return library books
- Ask John if he wants a ride
- Check bike tire

WHERE? HOW?

Words can be written on paper, on canvas, on wood, or on rocks. They can be written with pencil, with ink, or with paint. They can be carved or scratched on trees, clay, bricks, stone, or concrete. They can be written by hand or typed on a keyboard.

Keeping Our Words

We have seen how spoken words, unless recorded, are lost. Being able to record sound is very new, not even *150 years old*. Written words, though, can last for as long as the surface on which they're written lasts. If the *paper* or *wood* doesn't rot, the marks remain. If the paints and inks don't fade, the marks remain. If the rock surfaces are not damaged, *the marks remain.*

FOR EVER & EVER

Let's think about these ancient marks for a minute. If the marks remain, and those marks are very old, could that be important? You bet it is! We talked about how language changes. We know that there are many languages in the world, spoken by people of many different cultures. We also know that countless ancient cultures have disappeared. Could there possibly be records of these languages that have not been discovered yet?

A PICTURE IS A THOUSAND WORDS

Prehistoric people painted pictures on cave walls, mostly of animals. There are examples of these drawings, in different parts of the world, which are forty thousand years old. We aren't exactly sure why these were done, but we do know that humans like to communicate. What were these people saying? What did their speech sound like? See if you can find out more.

ANCIENT WRITING

Some early cultures did use a sort of writing, though. They wrote in pictures because they had not developed an alphabet yet. These *pictographs*, which can also be called *pictograms*, were the very first types of writing. They were done much later than the cave paintings, but by then the pictures had become symbols for words. The people who made them wanted to express their ideas, just as we do.

BIG WORD ALERT!

Here's another one for your collection: *cuneiform*.

Cuneiform was the first form of writing, and is about 3,500 years old. It was very basic, and used a more advanced type of pictographs. Wedge-shaped marks were made with a reed on wet clay tablets, which were then baked. The system was used for thousands of years by several cultures in the Middle East.

Several million of these clay tablets have been found, but so far few have been decoded and read. The tablets may be the first data files, and experts continue to work on understanding the valuable information they contain. With these tablets, humans took a large step toward communicating ideas and information in writing. Humans had learned to *save* their words.

Hello, Hieroglyphs

Wide word alert! About 3,500 years ago, Egyptians began using a system of *pictures* and *letters* called *hieroglyphs* to record facts. Hieroglyphs were carved and painted on rocks, walls, and other materials. Objects made of clay, such as jugs, were decorated in hieroglyphs, and became *beautiful* as well as useful.

TUT! TUT!

Stunning wall paintings have been found in ancient Egyptian tombs. The hieroglyphs tell stories about the people buried there. You've probably heard of King Tut, and you probably know that his name is Tutankhamen. *Tut* is easier though, don't you think? He still thrills the world after all this time. Can you find out more about him?

GOT ANY PAPER?

The ancient Egyptians worked out how to make a heavy kind of paper from the papyrus plant. This was an invention of huge importance. People called *scribes* were able to write in hieroglyphics on papyrus scrolls. The writings took practice and time, but the scrolls could be rolled up and saved. Examples of these ancient papyrus scrolls were first discovered in 1752.

At first, scholars could not understand the letters and signs, so the language of the scrolls remained a mystery. Less than fifty years later, in 1799, Napoleon's soldiers in Egypt dug up an ancient stone with three kinds of writing carved into it. This incredible find was the key to unlocking the language of hieroglyphics.

THE ROSETTA STONE

This partly broken black stone, which gets its name from the place it was found, contains the same message in three different texts. Ancient Greek is one of them, and was easy for experts to understand. The Greek writing made it possible to decode the ancient language of the hieroglyphics.

All the writings on the walls of tombs, and all the scrolls could now be translated. The history of ancient Egypt has not been lost. The constant work of archaeologists brings it back to life. Did you know the Rosetta stone came from the ruins of an ancient temple? Why? The stones were used to build a new fort. This must be one of the most important bits of recycling ever!

Do You Know Your ABCs?

Many of us can remember being asked this question when we started school. Most, but not all, languages have a written form. Sets of *signs*, called letters, are used to *write* words. These letters stay the same, and the words written with them take the place of spoken words.

THE WONDERS OF AN ALPHABET

αβ

Before you can write words correctly in your own language, you need to know your alphabet. The word *alphabet* comes to us from the first two letters of the Greek alphabet, which are *alpha* and *beta*.

Once an alphabet is learned, a world of information and communication opens. You can read and write a language, of course, but perhaps the best part is making words. The twenty-six letters of the English alphabet can be arranged, endlessly, to make thousands of words.

THE LONG & SHORT OF IT

There are about forty-six alphabets still used in the modern world. The English alphabet has fewer letters than some, but it's longer than the Greek alphabet, which has twenty-four.

អក្សរក្រមខ្មែរ

The largest alphabet is the Cambodian, which has seventy-four letters and is used by about eight million people!

Rotokas, the language of an area in New Guinea, has only twelve letters. Rotokas is spoken by fewer than five thousand people and is in danger of disappearing forever.

Αα Ββ Γγ Δδ
Εε Ζζ Ηη θθ
Ιι Κκ Λλ Μμ
Νν Ξξ Οο Ππ
Ρρ Σσς Ττ Υυ
Φφ Χχ Ψψ Ωω

ALPHA BRAVO CHARLIE

What's that? These are the first letters of a very important English alphabet. Big word alert! The *International Phonetic Alphabet* (IPA) was created in the 1950s to be used in voice communications, such as radio and telephone. It uses all the letters of the English language to spell out words. Radio operators, police officers, and pilots, among others, use this spelling system. Will you try to learn this alphabet? You and your friends could have great fun.

Phonetic alphabet

Alpha	**B**ravo	**C**harlie	**D**elta	**E**cho	**F**oxtrot
Golf	**H**otel	**I**ndia	**J**uliet	**K**ilo	**L**ima
Mike	**N**ovember	**O**scar	**P**apa	**Q**uebec	**R**omeo
Sierra	**T**ango	**U**niform	**V**ictor	**W**hiskey	**X**-ray
		Yankee	**Z**ulu		

MAKE NO MISTAKE

It's easy to misunderstand words spoken through an instrument, especially if there's noise or the speaker has an accent. In an emergency, misunderstandings can be a matter of life or death. For example, the pilot of a plane registered as G-KELS, would say: "This is golf kilo echo lima sierra, requesting permission to land."

They've Got Character

Glyphs are symbols, called characters, used to write some languages. We discussed the glyphs of the ancient Egyptians. Do you remember what they are called? *Chinese*, the most spoken language on Earth, uses glyphs, too. The glyphs represent whole words, and parts of sentences. Japan and Korea use slightly changed versions of the Chinese system to write their languages.

LOST & FORGOTTEN

Languages with no written form will eventually vanish. If there's no record of a language, it will become extinct when it is no longer spoken. Well, you might say, should we be concerned if there's nobody left to speak it? Does it really matter?

A TERRIBLE LOSS

If no one speaks a particular language anymore, should we care? Yes, indeed. When a language dies, we lose all the knowledge it contains. All the history of the culture and its people is lost. Fields such as science, linguistics, and the arts lose. Valuable information is gone forever, especially if the language had no written form.

SCARY

We know that about seven thousand languages are spoken in the world. Experts predict that more than 50 percent of these, and maybe as many as 90 percent of all languages, will be extinct by the end of this century. Should we be doing something about it?

A SPECIAL LANGUAGE . . .

Before the Europeans began to arrive in the Americas, there were thousands of native languages spoken. Today many of these languages have vanished completely, and many more are in grave danger of disappearing. The Cherokee language is still spoken by between thirteen and twenty thousand people. Although that's a very small number of native speakers, Cherokee does have a writing system, which has helped to preserve it.

. . . AND A VERY SPECIAL PERSON

Sequoyah, a learned man of the Cherokee tribe, developed a *syllabary* for the language. This big word for your collection means a set of characters forming part of the sound of a word. His language was so important to him that he worked for years to develop this writing system for his people.

Losing Languages

Many languages have already been *lost*, and many are in great danger of *extinction*. Huge changes in the world can cause populations to shrink, so that fewer and fewer people speak the language of their culture. *Wars* frequently change language maps. When the last native speaker dies, so does that language.

NOT ALLOWED

Can you imagine being forbidden to speak in your native language? Sadly, this has happened for centuries. People have been severely punished, and even killed, for speaking in their mother tongue. It's hard for us to understand such a terrible thing.

When countries were attacked, the invaders often tried to ban the local languages so the conquerors would have more control over the population. The Ottoman Empire banned the people of Albania from writing in their native language, for example. The English-speaking settlers in Australia prevented the Aboriginal peoples from speaking their languages, and most of these languages have been lost as a result.

DEAD, BUT NOT GONE

Languages no longer spoken are referred to as dead languages, although some of these languages are still studied and used. Ancient Greek and Latin, which we call classical languages, are examples. Because these have a written form, they are preserved. Ask any doctor, lawyer, or scientist just how important Greek and Latin are in his or her work. Voices from long, long ago still speak to us.

INVENTING WORDS

Can you make up a new word and get your friends to use it? Would it be difficult to do? Imagine if you created a word that would be listed in dictionaries. It could happen, but first you need to get many people to use it. Getting many people to use just one word isn't easy to do. So could a whole language be invented?

Wogglejog   Flibknit   Yumplish   Zapperfly

Zinglezap   Blingbat   Mizzlegrump   Slobyob

Bugfuzzed   Blingbat   Mizzlemouth   Creepydeep   Wanglecreep   Zapperhog

Fusslepants   Backyab   Scrabdab

INVENTING LANGUAGES

26TH JULY
THE DAY OF

Esperanto

— SINCE 1887 —

A new language, called *Esperanto*, was invented in 1887 to be a second language for people from different countries. Esperanto has a simple set of rules and is not very hard to learn. It allows people to communicate through a common language. Would you like to try it? Could be interesting. Look up Esperanto on the web and get started!

Why Learn?

Should people try to learn new languages? Absolutely! Seize every chance to learn even a few words of another language. Why learn now? Because younger brains usually learn new languages faster than older brains. A new language expands your *brain*, makes travel *easier*, and opens your world to new friends and experiences. You'll be a more *interesting* person, and it certainly helps when *job* hunting.

GREAT TO TRANSLATE

If you can translate even a little from one language to another, you'll be very popular when your pals or other people need help interpreting something.

Professional translators, whose work is translating a language into speech or the written word, are experts in all parts of the foreign language. Some professional translators specialize in one specific type of translating, such as computer engineering or French cooking.

CODE TALKERS

Bilingual speakers of languages known only to a few people are of enormous importance during wars. They can send messages, or cross enemy lines, using their native language. During the Second World War, Native Americans in the US Marines who could speak the Navajo language worked in code. This was absolutely vital to transmit secret information.

MAN & MACHINE

Computer software can translate just about all languages. It does so very precisely, often choosing the wrong words, and without the finer points of grammar and human speech. "He threw a stone at me," might be translated from one language to another as: "He threw me with a stone."

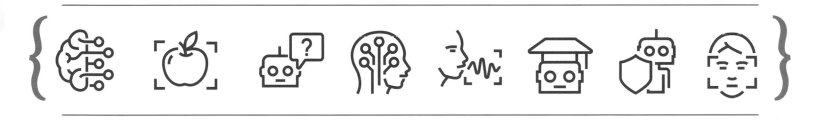

ROBOT SPEAK

Computer programs allow people who cannot speak to express themselves through artificial speech. The words are entered into the computer to be translated into sound. Various speaking voices can be used to utter the words, which can then be heard by others. This modern advance literally gives a voice to those who cannot speak.

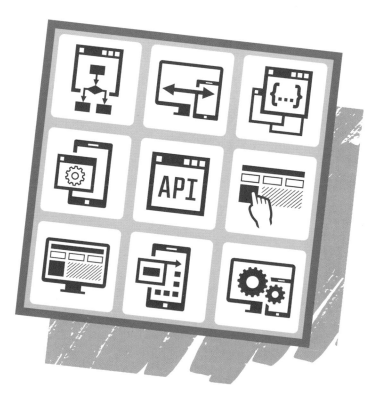

Language Talks

Language, and how we use it, tells us a great deal about the person or people speaking. It's not just the words themselves that carry meaning. Is the speaker using his or her mother tongue? Is the person confident or nervous? Is the speaker respectful? Does he or she swear? If the person uses slang or jargon, can we understand it? We can learn a lot from the way people speak.

TONE IT DOWN

The speaker's tone of voice can say a great deal more than his or her words. Is the person speaking politely, in a pleasant voice? Is he or she snarling? Shouting? Sarcastic? An ugly tone strikes a very ugly note. And by the way, have you noticed that *tone* and *note* have the same letters? Good for you!

SLANG

Do you use *slang*? That word has such a nice ring to it, but what does it mean? Slang refers to words not part of the formal language. By formal language we mean the standard version of a language.

For people studying a new language from books and tapes, slang can be hard to learn. The words may make no sense in the way they are used. It can also put a non-native speaker in some embarrassing situations.

WHERE DID THAT COME FROM?

Each country and each language group has its own slang. The slang words of some countries can be so good — and seem so right — that other countries begin to use them, also. Think of the phrase *couch potato*. Isn't that a perfect way to describe a particular type of person? What other slang words and phrases do you know?

OUT OF DATE

Slang changes all the time. The slang your parents used likely means nothing to you. Language is a living thing, and grows to fit the needs of the people who speak it. These changes make language so very interesting.

Jargon

The term *jargon* refers to special words used between people who share a common interest such as a type of work or *hobby*. If you play video games or a sport, for instance, you probably know all about jargon. Jargon can be a great communication *shortcut* for people in the know, saving both time and words. People who aren't in the know usually don't like a group's jargon because it can be very *confusing*. Slang and jargon are not the same.

SOMETHING TO EAT?

If you use the Internet, you know about spam. You may love the Spam that comes in a can, but having your inbox clogged with spam is most irritating. Let's make fun of Internet spam, and yell, "Can it!"

SOMBRERO

Sombreros are a type of hat, right? Yes and no. To soccer players, *sombrero* is jargon for a particular move that sends the ball over an opponent's head. Let's play a bit more, shall we? To a great soccer player, we could say, "I take my hat off to you."

WHERE'S THE TRAIN?

Those who travel by train stand on a platform. You may never get on a train, but if you play video games, you know what a platform is. Jargon can be quite confusing to people who aren't involved in the activity. (*Jargon* is an old word. See if you can find out the original meaning.)

FOLKS WHO JOKE

Some people love to make puns, which are plays on words. The origin of the word *pun* is not clear, but we do know that it's been used in English since the 1600s. It's an easy word to remember, though, because it rhymes with . . . ? *Fun,* of course!

VERY PUNNY

There are endless ways to play with words and make puns. Have you heard the one about fish? No? Here goes then: *The best way to communicate with a fish is to drop it a line.* Do you like tomatoes? What about this one? *How can you mend a broken tomato? With tomato paste.* Here's another funny thing about puns. People always seem to groan when you make one, but you know what? They love them!

Where Are You from?

People from foreign countries tend to have an accent, and may sound different from us. It's very difficult to pronounce foreign words correctly when you didn't learn them at a young age. How many of us can speak more than one language?

SOUNDS A BIT FUNNY

Native speakers of the same language may also have an accent. "Oh, he's from the north," we might say of someone who grew up in a different part of our own country. Do people from outside your area sound like you when they speak? What examples of regional accents can you think of?

DIALECTS

Speaking in a *dialect* is not the same as simply having an accent. Dialects have words and grammar that the standard language form does not. They can be very difficult to understand for newcomers.

WHY? WHERE? WHO?

Dialects develop where people are separated in some way from the main language group. Mountains and valleys, rivers, lakes, and seas cut people off. It wasn't easy to travel in bygone times, and still isn't even today in some parts of the world.

Differences in social class can lead to dialects arising, too. Speaking in dialect unites a group, and outsiders are noticed because they don't speak the local version of the language.

WHEN?

It takes time for a dialect to form. Ancient Greeks, for example, spoke several dialects, and scholars know about a few of them from texts on gravestones. Greece has hundreds of islands, where modern Greek is spoken in different dialects.

WHO DECIDES?

Can we really say that speaking our own language with a particular accent is better than someone else's accent? The most important thing is to be understood. Radio and TV news reporters usually speak with a more standard or neutral accent for that reason.

MIND YOUR MANNERS

Sometimes silly people make fun of the way other people speak. They mock accents and mistakes. That's very bad manners, and such behavior shows ignorance.

BIG WORD ALERT!

Some people have a *speech impediment*, which means they can't speak clearly, or they have trouble saying words. An example is stuttering, where the speaker stumbles over his or her words. Be patient. No one's perfect.

No Words

Speaking is so much a part of our lives that we seldom think about it. Humans can communicate in many ways *without* using their voices, though. *Signs,* symbols, and *gestures* can say a lot . . . without saying a word.

CAN'T TALK NOW!

Sometimes, you can't talk even if you want to. You can't speak if you are underwater, for example, or when your phone has no signal, or when your teacher is explaining a lesson. In times of danger, it may be safer not to make any noise. Other times, you may be trying to talk, but the listener doesn't speak your language or cannot hear you.

SIGNING IN

Have you noticed that sometimes on TV there's a person making signs with his or her hands? This person is using sign language to translate the words of a speaker for people who cannot hear.

HANDY!

Signing is a system of signals made with hands, fingers, the face, and body movements. Just as with spoken language, there are several different sign languages. There can even be dialects of sign language.

MOMMY! DADDY!

Have you seen a baby holding out its arms to be picked up? This sign clearly shows what the baby wants. Some parents teach their babies signs that may help their young children talk with their hands. Baby sign language isn't for young babies, though. Most children need to be about eight months old before they can sign.

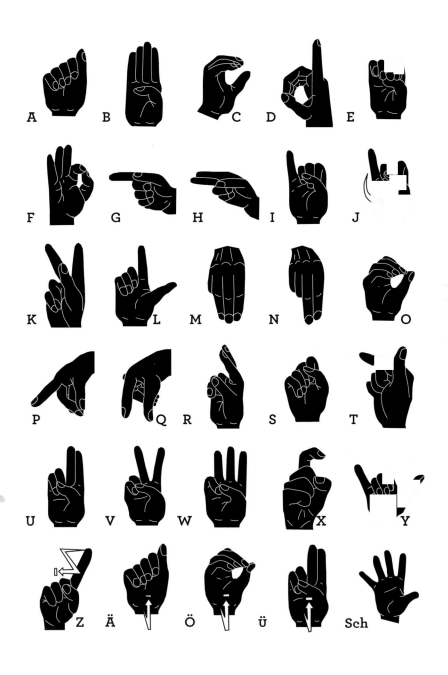

See What I'm saying?

People of all cultures and all *language* groups use body language to express some kind of meaning. People who are very *happy* and *excited* may run around, jumping up and down, smiling and laughing. Those who are watching know that all is well.

BUT . . .

Sad people, or people in pain, may stay very still. Sometimes they curl their bodies up tightly, or wrap their arms around themselves. They may cover their heads, or bury them in their hands. They may not want to look up. Their bodies tell how bad they are feeling.

ARM ALARM

Many messages can be sent through the way people position their arms. Someone waving his or her arms about may be warning of danger.

You can usually tell if your parents or teachers are not happy about something, can't you? There's that look on their face, but if they stand with their hands on their hips, or fold their arms across their body as well, you get the message.

WITH OPEN ARMS

We may throw our arms up in shock, or wide open in welcome. We may put our arms around each other to say hello and good-bye.

We hug when we're happy, and when we're sad. A hug can say we're so sorry for something we've done, or for something that's happened to a person. Hugs often speak more loudly than words to show how much we care. There's no need to speak when a hug does all the talking for you.

GIVE ME A HAND

We have already seen how important hands are in sign languages of the deaf. Let's look at some other hand signals and their typical meanings. Police direct people and vehicles with certain gestures. Holding the hand up, palm out, means STOP. There's probably no place in the world, whatever the language, where this signal would not be understood. No need to say a word.

SHAKE! SHAKE!

We shake hands with other people for many reasons. It could be we've just met, or are saying good-bye. Maybe we're shaking hands to seal a deal. People might shake hands after an argument, to say they are sorry. Hand shaking has a very long history, and probably was used to prove someone didn't have a weapon.

A FISTFUL

In more recent times, the fist bump shows that we agree with someone, or that we're pleased to see him or her. It's a way of showing respect. When a clenched fist is shaken at someone, though, it's usually a sign of anger.

A SLAP

The high five, where we slap open hands together, is another sign that all is well. It shows we like the other person or that we're pleased about something. It can say "Well done!" without using any words. As you know, a slap meant to hurt a person is something else entirely.

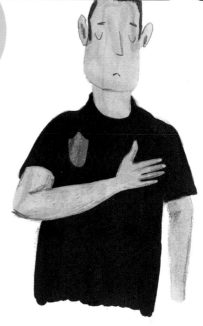

We may put our hand over our *heart* to show we are *sincere* and mean what we say. Many cultures do so, as a mark of respect, when their national song or anthem is played. Sometimes this gesture is used as a *silent* sign of sympathy, or to show *understanding*.

A GENTLE TOUCH

Placing a hand on someone's arm or shoulder can express our feelings without us saying a word. We may do it to show we're sorry about something, or it could be we are concerned and care about the person.

Other times, we may touch someone as a gentle warning to stop doing something, or to get his or her attention.

RESPECTFULLY

Placing the hands together with open palms can be a sign of respect, or may mean that help is needed. Showing the hands like this can also be used to indicate that no harm is intended. The person may also bow or bend his or her head while making this gesture.

SPORTING GESTURES

Hand signals are very important in some sports. Referees and other officials use their hands to control the game. There's no need to speak. They might not be heard anyway, but the players can see the signals and know what they mean. How many referee signals do you know?

HAND IT TO ME

Coaches and players may decide among themselves what gestures to signal to each other during a game. These signs are worked out during team practices and are considered top secret.

ON THE OTHER HAND . . .

Rival teams will be on the alert, trying to work out the secret hand signals their opponents are using. Each team is trying to gain the upper hand.

Very Handy

If you're in a place where you can't speak the language, your *hands* can say a lot for you. You may *point* to your stomach and mouth if you're looking for a place to eat. You can indicate a spot on a map as a way of *asking* for directions.

PUT YOUR HANDS IN THE AIR

Sometimes, when we're confused, we throw our hands up in the air as if to say, "I give up."

OH, MY

Covering your mouth with your hand can mean several things. It can show that you're too shocked to speak. Or maybe that you can't believe what you're hearing or seeing. It could also be a sign that you're not going to say anything, or that you do not agree with something.

CLAP, CLAP, CLAP

Clapping the hands together is common to all cultures and can say many things. It's a clear sign that we like something or are very pleased. It's also a way of getting someone's attention, to make them listen or to stop them from talking. An audience may also clap along in time to music they are enjoying.

MOCKING

Clapping slowly is not always a good sign, though. It might mean that people are bored, or tired of waiting. It might be sarcastic, meaning that the audience does not think much of what they're seeing or hearing.

NORTH OR SOUTH?

People often use their hands when they talk. Some linguists believe that people from certain countries do this more than others. They point out that people from warmer countries in southern Europe, such as Greece, Italy, and Spain, gesture quite a bit when they speak. People from the colder, northern countries tend to use their hands less. Have you noticed what people do with their hands when they're talking?

YOU THINK?

Does this mean anything? Maybe yes, maybe no. Warmer climates make it easier to be out and about, so perhaps that makes people happier. Maybe it's because people in the north are bundled up tightly in their clothes, so it's hard to wave their hands about. It depends on the person really, doesn't it?

What other hand signals can you think of? There are hundreds of different hand signs used around the world. Have you seen some that you don't know? Be careful and mind your hands! A hand signal you use may mean something completely different in another country. You certainly don't want to cause any trouble.

A BIG NO-NO

Holding your hand up, with the fingers spread far apart and the palm facing away from your body, is an extremely insulting gesture in Greece. (It's similar to the classic STOP signal, but the fingers are not kept together.) Take care never to do this! Greeks will be very tolerant of foreigners as a rule, but there's no need to give even a hint of offense.

OKAY? MAYBE NOT

Placing the thumb and forefinger together in a circle, with the other fingers raised, is used in most parts of the world as a positive sign to mean that all's well. A word of warning, though: this non-verbal sign can offend people in certain countries, where it has negative meanings. Making this sign to a person can mean he or she is a zero, or worth nothing.

GOT TO GO!

Whether you call it bathroom, toilet, WC, or a restroom, we've all needed one at some time or another. Thank goodness for signs all over the world that make it clear through pictures that you've found what you need.

MY HOUSE, MY STREET

Take a quick look around your neighborhood. There are likely to be many signs, such as Beware of the Dog, No Parking, Home Alarm System, Kids Play Here, Keep Out!, and a great many more. What signs can you spot?

MY CAR

What about the signs that people put on their cars? You may learn something from bumper stickers and other signs. Is there a Baby on Board? Is the driver handicapped? Does the driver support a particular group? License plates have information about the region the vehicle comes from. These signs are very interesting as long as nearby drivers don't become too distracted.

HIGHWAY CODES

Many kinds of symbols and signals are used in road traffic signs all over the world. Some signs give warnings, others information. All warning signs must be obeyed. To ignore them is very foolish, not to mention dangerous. Drivers must be aware of what the signs mean, especially if they're driving in a foreign country.

Top secret

Do you have special hand *signals*, which only your friends and family understand? When and where do you use them? Have some *fun* and see if you can work out new ones.

CAREFUL

What if someone wags a finger at you? It may be a warning, or it may be in fun, but it definitely sends a message. It's a message without spoken words, and it's up to you to work it out. There may be clues in the person's body language. Is the person relaxed or tense? His or her face may say it all through a smile or very tight lips.

SSSHHH!

We all know what's being said when people put their finger on their lips. We understand at once that we should be quiet, whatever the reason. Maybe there's danger. Maybe there's a need to hear something better. It could be we're just too noisy, or talking too much. Perhaps it's a warning not to repeat what you've heard. Even though no word has been spoken, the meaning is clear.

WHO? ME?

Using the index finger to call someone over to you is another commonly used sign. We refer to this as *beckoning*. The finger curls toward the person making this sign. This sign can also be used to catch someone's attention.

AND YOUR POINT IS?

Pointing your finger at someone is considered very rude in some countries. So is beckoning. Be careful, and respect local customs if you are traveling in a foreign land.

FINGERS CROSSED!

We often do this when hoping for good luck, or that something doesn't go wrong. However, it's considered very impolite in certain countries.

Watch Those Thumbs

Holding the thumb up is commonly used to indicate that all is well. The opposite is true if the thumb points down. See what you can find out about the origin of these signals, which come to us from the ancient Romans. But be careful and, yes, you've guessed it. The thumbs-up sign is an absolute no-no in certain countries.

GOING MY WAY?

The thumbs-up sign is also used by hitchhikers who want to catch a ride.

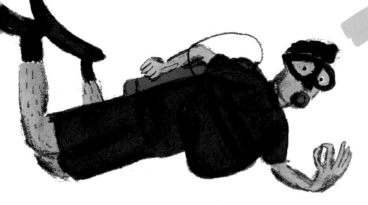

HEADING UP

Underwater divers use thumb signals differently to show other divers what they intend to do. In this case, thumbs-up means the diver will rise up in the water. Thumbs-down means the diver intends to dive deeper.

Hand signals are very important to those divers who have no voice communication in their equipment. These signals can mean the difference between life and death.

THUMB BITERS

In former times, to bite your thumb at a person meant that you despised him or her. It was often a sign that you wanted to get into a fight. Today it's more likely to suggest someone is nervous.

TAP, TAP, TAP

Tapping your fingers, your hand, or your foot can say all kinds of things without any words. It may mean you're bored, or angry. You may do it to get someone's attention, or to tell people to hurry up.

FIDGETY FEET

Shifting from foot to foot is often a sign that the person's getting restless. It could mean he or she is not comfortable, or wants to leave. The next time you're waiting in a long line, check out the feet of the people in front of you. How many people are shifting from foot to foot?

STAMPING

People may clap and stamp their feet when they really like something they're watching, such as a performance. Sometimes, though, stamping is part of a temper tantrum, especially in people who can't express their feelings better. It's one thing for a little child to do it, but it's not what we expect of others.

LOOK OUT

Stamping the feet can be a warning sign of anger or danger. Warriors used foot stomping to work themselves up before rushing into a battle.

It's All in Your Head

Your *head* and how you *move* it say quite a bit. In most countries, shaking the head from side to side means *no*, and nodding it up and down means *yes*.

WAIT!

Before you head off to foreign countries, take note. In Greece, Turkey, Bulgaria, and others, these head movements mean the exact opposite. In some cultures, moving the head up sharply means no. Moving it from side to side means . . . well, you get it. It means yes.

UP & DOWN

Nodding your head while someone is speaking shows that you are listening, or that you agree. We may also nod when greeting someone, or to indicate we've heard him or her. Nodding at a person serving in a restaurant, for example, tells the server we need something.

UP

"Chin up!" we say to cheer a person up. Holding your head up high lets others see that you're okay, whatever the situation may be.

Bowing your head and then raising it to look at the other person or persons is a sign of respect in many cultures. Here your body language will show that you're confident, and not afraid or upset.

DOWN

Hanging your head down is quite the opposite, and may show shame or sorrow. People who do this could be very distressed or frightened.

Holding your head to one side may show that you don't understand. Or it might be a way of asking the person to repeat what was said.

SO . . . ?

You shrug when you raise your shoulders up to your head. It's easy to understand this common, non-verbal signal. It could be saying that the person doesn't care what others think. It could be saying, "Nothing to do with me!" Sometimes, to make the point even more strongly, the arms are raised with the hands turned outward.

Let's face It

Your face is part of your *head*, and it has your eyes, your nose, your mouth, and tongue. All of these body parts can *communicate emotions* without you saying a word. Or maybe not. Some people can control themselves so well that we can't guess what they're thinking. We call this a poker face, or having a deadpan expression.

AYE EYES

Much has been written over the centuries, in every culture, about the eyes. It's quite true that our eyes can tell others a lot, without a word being spoken. When we laugh and smile, our eyes crinkle up and are said to sparkle. But when a person's smile doesn't match his or eyes, a keen observer knows the smile is false.

WHAT SAY YOUR EYES?

Our eyes may become narrow when we're angry, or when we're deep in thought. We may frown, as well. Eyes often open wide if we are surprised or shocked, or if we are terrified. People tend to blink rapidly if they are nervous, fearful, or trying to decide what to do.

WHO ARE YOU STARING AT?

We might stare hard at a person to show that we're annoyed or don't believe him or her. It can also be a signal that says, "Go away." It might let the other person know he or she is disliked, or challenges that person to say or do something. Being stared at makes people feel uncomfortable. Don't believe it? Try it with your friends and see what happens.

EYE CONTACT

The way we look into people's eyes is called *eye contact*. Looking hard into another person's eyes might be saying, "Believe me!" Refusing to meet another person's eyes could mean that the person is uneasy. His or her eyes might move from side to side, as if the person's looking for a way to escape. Some people avoid eye contact because they are very shy.

OH, PLEASE

Closing your eyes at someone might show that you're bored, or that you're not listening. We may roll our eyes if someone has said or done something stupid, showing that we don't believe what we're hearing, or we're annoyed. Rolling the eyes when someone's speaking is not considered a polite thing to do.

BROW SPEAK

Our eyebrows have spoken for us long before speech. When people pull their eyebrows together in a frown, we know they're not pleased, or they're puzzled. Raising the eyebrows is a way of silently asking a question. It may also show surprise, or even anger.

SOMETHING TO HIDE?

Have you noticed that the bad guys in movies often wear dark glasses? Is that so people can't tell where they're looking? Of course, there are many times when dark glasses are worn for perfectly good reasons. Can you think of some? And don't forget, body language can give clues about a person.

The Sign of the Nose

Sounds like a book title, doesn't it? Touching a *finger* to the *nose* has various meanings in different societies. The person doing it might be keeping a *secret*. It can also be used as a *private* signal. For example, someone might say, "When I touch my nose, we'll leave."

HMMMM . . .

Placing your index finger on your nose and thumb under your chin could show that you're thinking hard. It could also be a sign that you're not going to speak.

HELLO!

Some cultures touch noses as a way of greeting, though we're not really sure how or why this tradition developed. Clearly, if you're rubbing noses, you are not enemies. Inuit people, the Maori of New Zealand, people in Hawaii, people in Mongolia, and others touch noses.

SNIFFY

We often wrinkle our noses if we don't like the smell or taste of something, or we're disgusted. We may do it if we're not happy about something, or are puzzled and trying to decide what to do about a situation. If there's an awful smell, we might pinch our nostrils closed. No words needed!

MY NOSE KNOWS

In some societies, tapping your nose is a way to show a particular person is not to be trusted. Perhaps this gesture has something to do with saying, without any words, "I smell trouble."

MIND YOUR MOUTH

Smiling is a sign of happiness, but curling your lip into a sneer indicates annoyance, or a lack of respect. Sneering is very bad manners in any culture. Pouting your lips is usually a sign of annoyance.

What about biting your lip? Perhaps you don't want to speak at all. It could signal stress or fear, but it certainly does say something to anybody watching.

Watch Your Tongue

There's so much more to *tongues* than shaping words. What do you think *clicking* your tongue might mean? **A horse** knows this signal, but what does it say to a human?

ACTING UP

Sticking your tongue out at someone is considered very rude in most societies. You may be making your feelings clear without bothering to speak, but it shows disrespect.

BUT NOT EVERYWHERE!

In Tibet, though, Tibetans put out their tongues a little as a greeting. They also use this gesture to show they agree with someone. This might seem strange to us, but don't forget that our ways may seem odd to other cultures.

DON'T MESS WITH US!

The Maori people of New Zealand stick their tongues out as far as they can when performing the Haka war dance. In the past, this behavior was used to frighten their enemies.

Have you seen the New Zealand rugby team perform the Haka at the start of a match? It's dramatic, and meant to show the other team that New Zealand intends to win.

speaking with silence

Not speaking at all can send a very **powerful** message. Together with the look on someone's face, silence can say many things. It might mean the person doesn't know, or doesn't care, or is scared. It could mean the **opposite**, in that the person is confident and doesn't need to **explain** his or her every thought.

NOISE ANNOYS

It's easy to talk, but quite difficult to stay quiet. Once we learn to speak, it seems we don't want to stop. We live in a world where we communicate constantly. We make so much noise.

Some communities value silence so much that it's a special part of their lives. In some religions, a time of silence is part of the everyday routine.

SILENCE SPEAKS LOUDLY

A lack of noise catches our attention very quickly. People marching, banging drums, or shouting protests are a common sight. Often we are hardly aware of them. People standing in silence, perhaps holding placards, are more likely to be noticed. It seems odd, doesn't it? Silence can send a very strong signal.

SILENT ENTERTAINMENT

Staying silent can be great fun, though. Have you tried it? Games where you're not allowed to speak are very amusing. Other players must guess what you're trying to be, or what you're saying. It's not that easy. You use every bit of body language you can, pulling all kinds of faces. Most of the time you're falling about laughing.

NO SOUND FOUND

Did you know that the earliest movies had no sound? People watched the actors on the screen, but there was no way yet to produce sound. Actors had to tell stories with face and body movements. Movie theaters used live piano players to set the moods: fast and dramatic piano playing for action scenes, and soft, gentle tunes for romance. Silent movies seem so funny to us now.

SUBTITLES!

Later, as movies began to improve, words would appear across the bottom of the screen for people to read. We still use subtitles on screens for deaf people, or to translate foreign languages. That's something you could try at home. Act out a scene, and hold up written signs to explain. Play some music. No spoken words allowed!

Special signals and words known only to certain people are *secret codes.* There are countless types of codes, but not all of them are secret. Codes are simply one way of communicating in a *non-vocal* manner. This means information can be shared without spoken words.

MORSE, OF COURSE

American scientist Samuel Morse developed what became known as the *Morse code.* This very important code sends signals over long distances, using wires, radio, sound, or light.

Letters of the alphabet and numerals are written as groups of long and short signals, called dots and dashes. Messages are sent by sounds such as tapping, drumming, buzzing, clicking, or flashes of light.

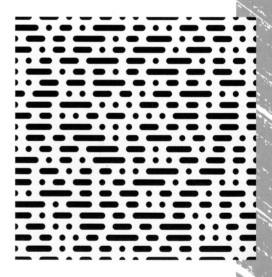

BATTERY PACK

MESSAGE RECEIVED

It takes a lot of skill and practice to send and understand Morse messages quickly. While Morse code is not as vital for communications today as it once was, it's still in constant use. Ham radio operators across the world use Morse code to talk without speaking. In times of disaster, Morse code is often the only means of life-saving communication.

WHAT DO YOU THINK?

Would it be fun to learn Morse code? Should you? Such knowledge is certainly good to have. You can even download an app that translates Morse code. Give it a try!

A WHOLE LOT OF DOTS

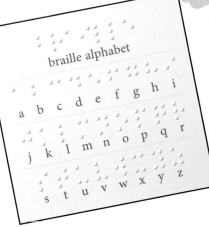

Braille is a code of raised dots that lets blind people read by touch. There are Braille systems for almost all languages, as well as for music, computers, and mathematics. Can you find out more about the inventor, Louis Braille, who changed the lives of those who cannot see?

COMPUTER SPEAK

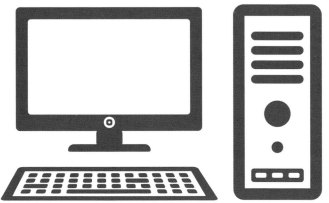

Computers talk to each other with a series of voltages that are either "on" or "off." Computers talk to nearby equipment such as keyboards and printers this way, also.

A number system that consists of only two possible values is called a *binary system*. A sequence or series of binary numbers can be coded to be anything we need: big numbers, letters, or even photographs.

⫸ More Codes ⫷

Sounds and colors have been used for centuries to send messages. The noise from striking wood, ringing bells, and blasting horns made important announcements. The group understood the messages, just as you know your school's sound system of bells and buzzers.

BANG! BANG!

Firecrackers and gunshots can be used to send signals. In countries where pirates often invaded in the past, a cannon was sometimes fired to warn people to seek safety. It could also be a message that the danger had passed, for example, and it was safe to come out. Each community would agree on a system of signals and what they meant.

SAY IT WITH COLOR

Pieces of cloth can be displayed or waved in a series of signals to send messages. The *semaphore system* of flag signals is widely used, with different flag colors for land and water communication. The people receiving these messages must be familiar with the code to understand the information being sent.

NO LIGHT AT NIGHT

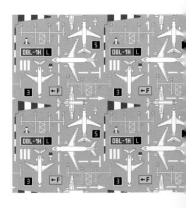

Perhaps it's already occurred to you that semaphore flags can't be seen at night? In that case, some kind of light is attached to the flagsticks, or special lighted wands are used.

QUITE PLAIN TO THE PLANE

If you've flown in an airplane, been at an airport, or even only watched a movie, you will have seen controllers on the ground. These marshals make signs with paddles to guide pilots. At night, or when visibility is poor, the paddles are lighted. The coded signals are vital instructions to the pilot, and could mean the difference between life and death.

FLAG IT

A red flag is known worldwide as a warning signal. International flag codes for shipping use particular colors and symbols to alert other vessels. The messages may indicate a problem, such as fire on board, or the need for medical help. Flags can also show other boats that a diver is nearby. This language of flags is not only interesting, but is a vital means of communication. Can you find out more?

DRESS SENSE

Clothing colors may show a person's status in a group. Purple became the color of royalty in ancient times because the dye was very hard to get and expensive.

Certain colors may be worn for special events in different cultures, such as wearing black for funerals. In many countries, brides wear white or ivory when they marry, but in other cultures, brides wear bright red. In areas of war and natural disasters, peacekeepers and aid workers wear certain colors so they can be easily seen.

Okay to smoke

Smoke signals have been a means of communication for a very long time. The ancient Chinese used smoke signals, as did the Greeks. Codes were worked out to *translate* the *puffs* of smoke. Important information could be sent over great distances, but windy weather must have been a *problem*!

NO SMOKE WITHOUT FIRE

Long before we had any of our modern ways to communicate over distances, fire was an important way of sending messages. A large fire would be lit, high up if possible, to say that an enemy was advancing, or that a victory had been won. To understand the message, the coded meaning had to be known by those who were receiving it.

BLACK OR WHITE

Smoke signals are still used today by the Roman Catholic Church in Rome. When a new pope is being chosen, the voting papers are burned after each vote. Black smoke indicates that no one has been elected yet. If the smoke is white, it means that the church has a new pope.

TALKING SMOKE

Many Native American tribes had their own language systems of smoke signals, and were expert messengers. The location the signal was sent from was also part of the code.

When a code was sent from a hilltop, for example, the meaning was different than if sent from lower ground. Whole chains of messages were transmitted back and forth this way.

The Body as Canvas

Tattoos have played a part in human life for thousands of years. Ancient *mummies* have them. Carvings in *wood*, on *rocks* and *vases*, and into stone show humans with tattoos, as do prehistoric cave paintings.

WHAT'S THAT TAT?

Why did our ancestors tattoo themselves? Tattoos were, and still are, cultural symbols. They are a permanent record of what was important to the person, and tell all kinds of stories. Long ago, criminals were given tattoos so they could easily be identified and always known for their misdeeds.

MARKS THE SPOT

Medicine men used tattoos when treating people. A wonderful example of this can be seen on the Iceman, named Otzi, who lived more than five thousand years ago. His mummified body was found in the Alps, and is carefully preserved in a museum. Scientists believe that various tattoos inked on his body probably referred to bone pain, and marked the places were he would have been treated.

HERE TODAY, GONE TOMORROW

Unlike tattoos, body painting is not permanent. Painting faces at parties and festivals is common now, but humans have painted their bodies from the earliest times. Tribes applied dyes and paints from plant materials, mud and clay, and animal and bird droppings. They added feathers, shells, bones, stones, bits of wood, and other items to pass on information.

The symbols painted on the body may give details of the person's age, tribe, and position in the group. Does he or she have children? Is the person a great hunter? A warrior? Body painting has been important to the Aborigines of Australia for thousands of years, and is a very serious form of communication.

SCARRED

You may have some scars on your body caused by an accident. Perhaps you were burned by something hot, or you were careless with a knife. Here's a word to add to your collection: *scarification*. It means making scars on purpose. Ouch! It sounds awful, but it was done in the past, and still is in some parts of the world.

Why on earth would anyone scar his or her body? Although it's hard for us to imagine, it would not have seemed odd to the tribe. Don't forget that signs and symbols were important in societies before writing was invented. Scars were permanent. Objects that showed status, such as necklaces, weapons, and tools, could be lost, but scars remained.

BEAUTY MARKS

Scarification is mostly seen in Africa, and bodies marked this way are considered very beautiful. The Zulu people of South Africa made cuts into their faces to pass on information. The number of cuts and their locations were important. Scars on the cheeks, the forehead, under the chin, and on the neck told stories about the person wearing them to those who knew the codes.

Mapping It Out

Humans have always been explorers. In ancient times, those who traveled far from home over land or by water were heading into the unknown. How very brave they were — for many centuries, people believed the earth was flat, and that people could fall off. Those who returned brought back wonderful stories and details of their journeys.

ROUGH IDEAS

As travelers collected information and made sketches of mountains and plains, seas and rivers, new and strange things would have been spoken about, again and again.

From these adventures, early maps were drawn. These maps were rough and nowhere near correct, but they had at least a bit of information. Have you ever tried to draw a map? What about one for a treasure hunt?

MAP IN HAND

As the centuries passed, further information was collected, and maps became more detailed. Rivers, seas, mountains, and valleys were shown and named. Maps often included drawings of monsters, pirates, robbers, and other dangers. Facts began to be written on them.

A traveler with a map is good to go, and needs no spoken words to find his or her way. Nowadays of course we have GPS, but maps are still beautiful things.

THE LANGUAGE OF MUSIC

People love music. Long before we could read and write, we passed music from generation to generation by memory. Sometime in the thirteenth century, musicians began to make marks showing details of notes to play or sing. This coded language is called *music notation* and is understood by all who play instruments, sing songs, and write music.

GETTING TO KNOW YOU!

Music groups or orchestras have a leader, called the *conductor*, who guides them with various hand gestures. Each conductor develops his or her own group of coded signals, which the musicians understand and follow. When a new conductor directs them, the musicians often have to learn a new set of signals. Imagine the racket if they didn't play together correctly!

YO!

Perhaps you've heard of *yodeling*, the type of singing that uses the voice at high and low pitches? It's mostly a form of entertainment now, but its origins lie in communication over long and difficult distances. We usually think of yodeling in Austria and Switzerland, where herders used it to call their animals, but yodeling is used in many other countries, too. It's a way to send messages between villages, and is still used quite a bit in Africa.

speaking with Things

Most of us have items that hold special meaning for us, such as a favorite collectible card, seashell, or jewelry. Maybe it reminds us of someone or some event in our lives. The owner may say, "It speaks to me," and the listener understands what he or she means.

THE ART OF A NATION

All cultures respect certain objects of great meaning to them. The Haida people of northwestern America occupy an area between British Columbia in Canada and Alaska. The Haida have been there for more than seventeen thousand years. They have a very long and important history, and are known for their striking totem poles.

LOGGING IN

Haida totem poles are very large logs, with signs and symbols carved on them. These beautiful totems stand outside of homes, or on some part of Haida land, and convey information of all kinds. The carvings carry messages for those who understand the coded language.

WOODEN HISTORY BOOKS

Totem poles spoke of many things. They recorded births and deaths. They carried greetings to those passing by in boats. Sometimes, they told of problems with other people, and gave warnings. The totem poles recorded the history of a culture.

BEFORE IT'S TOO LATE

Times changed, and the totems began to fall out of use. Many fell down and were left to rot. Now, though, people are seeing the value in such objects again, and what they represent. Totem poles are a non-verbal means of communication. In this day and age of so much noise, isn't that a good thing?

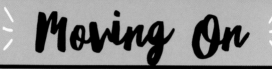

Moving On

Humans have moved from place to place, searching for food, since very ancient times. Tribes developed. Some settled in specific places. Others wandered far and wide and are known as *nomads*.

STICKS & STONES

From our earliest history, humans have passed on knowledge to others. Nomadic tribes, such as the Roma people traveling through Europe, marked their journeys by leaving signs.

Sticks and stones arranged a certain way left valuable information for others using the route. The codes were used to tell about important events, make meeting plans, and give warnings.

GRASS & BONES

Grass tufts were tied in certain ways to tell which direction to take. In desert areas, bones might be laid out in coded patterns, perhaps weighted down by rocks so animals wouldn't disturb them. Those outside of the group would probably not even have noticed these signs, but group members depended on these non-verbal communications.

FLY AWAY HOME

Messenger pigeons carry written messages in special little tubes fastened to their legs or backs. They can fly long distances, and are still used by police in some very remote areas where there is no telephone reception. Messenger pigeons can even deliver computer memory cards.

"The General will not arrive today."

"No travel due to landslide."

"I have won in Gaul!"
– Julius Caesar

"Send helicopter for the wounded."

"The enemy has captured the city. No postal service."

"The results of the yacht race are expected at noon."

"Medical supplies are low; we need bandages."

Picture It

Paintings as old as forty thousand years have been found in caves, though we are not sure exactly what these early artists were trying to say. What we do know is that people have always found ways to communicate their thoughts to others. You don't need to be an ancient caveman to do that. We've already seen how more modern people used systems such as cuneiform and hieroglyphics to record information.

THEN & NOW

Humans have always drawn pictures, and we still use them in every possible way today. Think about the emojis we use with phones and other devices. These little pictures speak as loudly as any words to say that we're happy or sad, angry or cheerful, and a great deal more besides.

You can send a whole story using only emojis. Have you tried it? Of course, if the person who receives your emojis story doesn't know the emoji code, he or she might have trouble understanding it.

TRADEMARKS

The golden arches of a certain food chain can be seen in more than a hundred countries, and there's no mistaking what they mean. Brand names and logos identify companies and their products, and can't be used by others without written permission. The trademark symbols of sports teams, schools, airlines, and shoemakers can be extremely well known and many people know them instantly by sight.

BIG WORD ALERT!

Here we go: *colophon*. You've seen many examples of these special marks but you probably didn't know it. Found on book spines and title pages, the marks have information about a book's publisher. The symbols can be made with pictures, letters, or words. Take a look at a row of books. How many colophons can you spot?

DANGER!

Have you already thought of the bone signal that's well understood by all language groups? No translation needed. The skull and crossbones warn of serious danger.

In every country, the skull and crossbones image means poison. If you understand the symbol, you do not need to use any language. Where else do you see the skull and crossbones?

CHAPTER 3 | Roar, Squeak, Animals Speak!

Let's Talk About Animals!

We've discussed the ways people pass on information to others about what we're thinking, what we know, and what we want. *Animals* communicate with each other. They exchange information with members of their own *species*, as well as other animals when needed. What kinds of *information* might animals pass on? Let's find out.

SENDING MESSAGES

Why should we talk about animals? Like us, they must make certain information clear. "Well," you might say, "I don't really need to talk to an ant. What can I discuss with an elephant? For that matter, why would a warthog want to speak to me?" It's quite funny about chatting with a warthog, but warthogs most certainly chat among themselves.

WARTS & ALL

African warthogs live in groups and roam in parts of Africa's grasslands. They are tough animals, but their survival depends on being in close touch with a group. Communication is essential to them. They share data, such as the locations of food and water. Remember, water can be scarce in Africa because droughts are common. Water also means mud, and warthogs love mud because it keeps them cool and protects their skin.

SO, WHAT'S HAPPENING?

Like many people, warthogs chatter a lot. They jabber in all kinds of sounds as they go about their lives. Snort, sniff, snuffle, squeak. They grunt; they growl; they mutter and mumble. Warthogs may look fearsome, but they have poor eyesight and don't look for trouble.

HELP!

When there's danger nearby, warthogs utter piercing warning squeals, and rush to the safety of their burrows. A warthog might get lost, or a baby warthog could wander away from its mother. Screaming and shrieking alerts the group to come to the rescue.

LET'S GET TOGETHER

Warthogs looking for a mate will call out in a particular way, and listen for a reply. As with many other animals, exchanging information is very important to warthogs — there's so much they need to know.

Sound Waves

Sound travels very well underwater, so some animals can send and receive information this way. Humpback whales communicate with each other with many sounds. The males sing songs, but only during mating season. The songs tell the females that a whale is fit and strong, and would be a good partner. Is he boasting? Maybe, but he has a lot of competition, and how else can the female choose?

DO WE KNOW YOU?

There are more than eighty species of whales, and each has a different sound. Whales can tell which species are near by the pitch of their whistles and calls. Like humans, each whale has a different voice. Biologists have found that whales from different areas of the oceans have different accents, too. Isn't this amazing?

WHERE ARE YOU?

Whale sounds can be heard over great distances. This communication allows them to stay close to their family, or pod. This is very important during their long migration journeys. Mothers can keep track of their babies, called calves, by calling to them. Whales communicate a great deal with the group, and with each other.

FISH TALES

Do fish talk? Male and female toadfish are able to make grunting sounds, and males whistle to call females to their nests. Some types of fish make different sounds at night than they do in the day.

GOING BATTY

Most bats are nocturnal, though a few species feed by day. Humans cannot hear the high-frequency sounds that bats use to communicate and navigate. These bat sounds are called echolocation. The word says it all: bats make high-pitched sounds that echo off objects and prey in their flight path so night-flying bats know where to go.

SUMMER SONGS

Cicadas have been known since the most ancient times. Only male cicadas make the summer sound we all know so well. They do this by flexing muscles in their abdomens. Why? It's to attract females and say, "I'm here. Where are you?"

Shall we play? We've all heard crickets chirping away, even though we don't always see them. Only male crickets chirp, hoping to attract a female. They make the noise by scraping their wings together. Their songs tell females what species they are and whether they're healthy.

Katydids are related to crickets and make sounds the same way. In a few species, female katydids answer male songs. Many katydids are so well camouflaged that they can be difficult to see. On summer nights, though, you may be able to hear their songs if you're in the right spot.

FROG SONGS

Like whales, birds, and many insects, frogs have unique songs, too. The males call out to females during mating season. Some frogs, such as the pig frog, are named after the animals they sound like.

Birds of a feather

Birds make such a large variety of sounds that the list of their noises is long. Birds sing and they shriek; they chatter, chirp, twitter, and trill. They whistle, whoop, coo, quack, caw, and warble. The sound may be pleasing, or it may ruffle your feathers. Birdsong communicates. That's what it's meant to do.

SING ME A SONG

As soon as day breaks, the bird concerts begin. Males do most of the singing, hoping that females will like what they hear. Some birds learn their songs by listening to neighbors and practicing. Other birds can sing their songs well without practice because they know the patterns through instinct.

HOOP-HOOP-HOOP

The beautiful hoopoe is not always easy to see, but its call is clear. The male sings his lovely hoop-hoop-hoop song early in the morning to attract a female to the nesting site. If the nest is threatened, the alarm call is different.

FLYING ACROBATS

Hummingbirds are the world's smallest birds. The males attract females in different ways. Some rotate their whole body to show wonderful colors in the sunlight. Males in dark forests chirp loudly together, so as to be heard. Other species swoop and dive at lightning speed to impress females. The females watch in silence, deciding which males to choose.

WHAT'S THAT I HEAR?

Listen carefully and you'll hear other bird noises. The singing changes to a different sound if there's danger. Alarm calls alert the birds and they'll fly off in a feathery flurry. Then you might hear one or two birds cheeping that it's safe to come back. A swoosh of flapping wings, and there they are again. They heard the message.

LISTEN UP

Communication between birds can be a matter of life or death. Parent birds hover about as their chicks learn to fly. They call constantly to them to keep them close and safe. If you watch parent birds teaching the youngsters, you'll soon hear the different calls they use. The chicks know what the parent bird is saying.

COME ON, LET'S GO!

Some bird species migrate with the seasons. Swallows, for example, gather in large clusters as they prepare to leave for warmer countries. It can take days before all the birds arrive at the departure point. With lots to tell, there's lots of noise. Then, the departure signal is given, and a great cloud of swallows soars into the sky. They're gone. The sudden silence is striking.

COME! EAT!

Many birds are very social and live in family groups, or flocks. They search all day for the worms, seeds, berries, fruit, insects, nectar, and other things they eat. When they find food, they call to the others and pass on the good news.

Noise Makers

Animals make so many sounds that no one can know them all. Dogs growl, cats purr, birds chirp, elephants trumpet, dolphins whistle, horses neigh, sheep and goats bleat, and so on, but not all animal sounds come from voices. Animals have other ways to make noises, just as we do. They can bang and stamp, and use body parts to create sounds that send signals.

PUTTING THEIR STAMP ON IT

Elephants have several ways to communicate, one of which is stamping their feet in a thunderous racket. When their heavy weight strikes the ground, it produces vibrations, which travel through the earth. These vibrations are picked up by the sense organs in the feet of other elephants and can warn them of danger, even from very far away.

SENDING OUT VIBES

From the enormous elephant to the tiny termite, some animals use vibrations to share information with other animals. How can a teensy termite make enough noise to warn its group of danger? One termite after the other will bang its head on the ground, and the message is relayed down the line. Quite amazing, no?

SHAKING & QUAKING

Spiders are very skilled in the language of vibrations. Have you ever noticed a spider lurking in its web? It doesn't need to see a fly, moth, or other juicy bit of prey land on the sticky strands. When a spider feels its silk threads vibrate, it knows dinner has been delivered, right to the door.

WELCOME!

Not all spiders live in webs, though. Trapdoor spiders live in holes they make in the ground. They weave silky threads across the entrance, creating a smart front door. Then they disguise the trap with plant material and wait in the comfort of their underground dwellings. When insects walk across the trapdoor, their vibrations tell the spiders underneath that dinner's on the table. Up they pop: "Come on in!"

RATTLE & SHAKE

The rattle on the rattlesnake's tail makes a special sound that says, "Beware!" Some other snakes also use their tails to send warning signals, but they do so by shaking their tail in a pile of leaves to create a noise.

Snakes do not have external ears and cannot hear the approach of a human or possible predator. Instead, they are very sensitive to ground vibrations, which warn them of danger. Snakes don't like you any more than you like them, so they usually slither quietly away.

ABOVE & BELOW

Hippos are thunderously loud animals. Bellowing males, defending their territory, can be heard for miles on land. They are just as noisy underwater, but the sounds can't be heard above water.

The Nose Knows

Noses are extremely important in the animal world, and are used for much more than simply smelling stuff. Newborn mammals, many of which can't even see yet, depend on their noses to find mom. Smell signals can also help lost animals find their way home or lead animals to shelter.

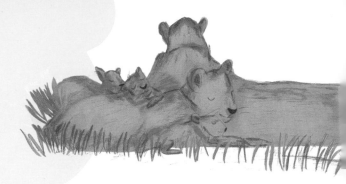

NOSE TO NOSE

Rubbing noses is a common way for many animals to greet each other. Dogs do it; horses do it; deer and pigs do it. Cats do it a lot. Special scent glands on their heads, noses, and cheeks let the animals learn about each other.

BIG WORD ALERT!

Here's a big word for you related to noses and sense of smell. It's an important word: *pheromones*. You say it like this: fare-oh-moans. These are chemical signals that animals give off, and which other animals of their species can smell and respond to. Pheromones signal food, water, danger, mates, and even weather changes.

NATURE'S ANTENNAE

Some moths, butterflies, and other flying insects use antennae to pick up signals from pheromones that may help them find food or mates. There are more than a thousand different types of insect pheromones. That's a lot of talking!

FORM A LINE, PLEASE

Have you ever watched ants moving in long lines, heading to and from food and water? If their nest is attacked, ants release pheromones to alert the others. Some ants will rush to protect the queen, while the rest go out to fight. Even something as tiny as an ant has non-vocal ways to pass on a message, and each knows what its job is. There are more than 10,000 species of ants, and each species has its own pheromone.

SCAT? WHAT'S THAT?

Scat is simply a word for poop. Poop is very important in the animal kingdom. Rhinos, for example, are huge animals, and so are their scat piles. Several rhinos use the same poop spot, trampling about in the mess. The smell tells them which rhinos have been there, and warns other rhinos to stay away. Yes, it's yucky to us, but it's their way of communicating.

Jackals and some other meat-eating animals hide their scent when they hunt. They roll in poop and smelly stuff to disguise their own odor. You could say they're concealing information. Phew!

WHAT'S THAT SMELL?

Some animals use liquids to mark their territory. The smell tells other animals to keep well away. We know what a terrible stink skunks give off when they spray to defend themselves. Yecch! Did you know that porcupines also send out awful smells?

Don't forget the little guys! Did you know that some millipedes also spray sticky, smelly stuff? Bombardier beetles don't play around in the smell game. They make a popping noise as they hurl out a truly horrible, vile-smelling mess. And they can do it again and again. Talk about dropping a bomb!

Broadcasting signals

An animal's head position says a lot. An animal with its head hanging down might be sick, or greatly distressed. An angry animal, such as a bull, lowers its head before charging. Rhinos have very poor eyesight and will often charge, head down, even though they might not be sure what they're thundering toward.

EYES FRONT

Some signals can be sent with the eyes. Humans think of staring as bad manners, but dogs will stare hard at a dog or other animal they don't like or want to warn off. Other animals do this too, often before attacking. Maybe your dog stares at you because he's trying to tell you something: "Let's go play."

FOOLING THE EYE

Some animals have markings called eyespots that look like eyes. These fake eyes may confuse predators. Eyespots are found on many animals, including butterflies, moths, fish, reptiles, birds, and cats. False eyes can also help attract mates. A beautiful example of eyespots is the male peacock's tail.

FALSE SIGNALS

Have you ever seen a stick insect? It looks exactly like a twig as long as it stays still. That's plan A for saving its life. Yes, there is a plan B. If a predator grabs it, it will shed one of its limbs to escape. But wait, if that fails, some types have a plan C. They can spray foul stuff at the enemy. The predator might finally get the message and give up.

TURN ON THE LIGHTS

Some animals can send signals in the dark. Have you seen bright little flashes of light at night? These could be fireflies sending messages to each other. There are about two thousand firefly species, and each one uses a different pattern of flashing light.

LYING LIGHTS

During mating season, male fireflies call out to females with light flashes. Females answer with their own flashes. In some species, males copy the light flashes of females in a nearby species. When the flashing male comes over, he finds a predator instead of a mate!

BIG WORD ALERT!

When animals make or use light, it's called *bioluminescence*. Many sea creatures use light, including some squid, fish, worms, and jellyfish. It's not done for fun, but rather to communicate vital information, such as the presence of predators. Flashing lights may also be a warning to the predators: "Watch out! I'm dangerous." Some animals use light to attract mates or prey, too.

A WORD IN YOUR EAR

Many animals raise their ears when alerted to noise. Animals may also twitch their ears as they try to interpret a sound, or lay their ears down flat when nervous or angry. Elephants flap their huge ears right before they charge. Look out!

MIND YOUR TONGUE

Lizards and snakes collect information with their tongues, too. Besides finding food, their tongues also smell pheromones left by other lizards. Look up the Komodo dragon, a fearsome-looking lizard with a long, forked tongue.

Non-Verbal Language

We've seen how humans, who have one body form, use body language. Animals use body language, too. What might animals want to tell each other? What are they telling us?

TUMMY TALK

When an animal rolls onto its back and shows its tummy, it's happy and relaxed. A fearful animal never exposes its abdomen as this is a very vulnerable part of its body.

I'M BIGGER THAN YOU THINK

Many mammals fluff out their tails and coats to look larger when something threatens them. Male lions puff out their beautiful manes to frighten other animals, while porcupines lift up their quills. These sharp quills spell danger better than any noises they can make.

What if a dog raises its hackles, the ridge of fur along his back? That shows he's angry or afraid. Cats also raise their hackles when alarmed or furious. It's easy to understand this clear warning sign.

WHAT BIG TEETH YOU HAVE

Many animals use their teeth to defend themselves, and not just by biting. They bare their teeth as a warning signal to others. Mandrills are the largest of the monkeys and are quite shy. The males have much longer canine teeth than the females, and dominant males have the longest canines. Bright red coloration on males also shows dominance.

CLACK ATTACK

Porcupines are active at night. When in danger, they clack and smack their teeth together to sound fierce. This is very useful in the dark, as the other animal doesn't know what kind of trouble it could be in.

WAGGLE! WAGGLE!

When a worker honeybee finds nectar, it returns to the hive to tell other bees. How does a bee share information? It uses a special group of movements called a waggle dance to tell others exactly where the food is. When the dance is finished, other bees buzz off, using the directions in the dance to find the nectar.

More Non-Verbal Language

With pets, it's usually easy to know what they want. Your dog fetches his ball to tell you it's time to play. He may push his food bowl around to let you know he's hungry. You understand each other because you know each other, and have worked out ways to communicate.

TELLING TAILS

Animals can send and receive much information through the language of their tails. The ring-tailed lemur holds its tail up to show the group where it's feeding. Males coat their tails with smelly stuff from their bodies and wave them about to let other males know who is boss.

Swishing the tail from side to side can mean anger, or that the animal is preparing to attack. Think of cats about to pounce on prey. Mind you, your pet cat is one thing, but a leaping lion is quite another. Deer raise their tails when alarmed, while squirrels flick theirs.

 PLAYING DEAD

Possums play dead to make predators lose interest. Some snakes use this trick, too, even making their bodies completely stiff. The southern hognose snake puts on a great dying act. The leaf litter frog will lie belly up, as if dead, to avoid being eaten. There are fish in east Africa that catch other fish by pretending to lie dead on the bottom. You could say they are dying to live.

SHOW OFF

The frigate bird is enormous. It lives mostly out at sea, swooping about in the winds. When the breeding season arrives, the male frigate bird inflates the red skin of his neck pouch to make himself attractive to females. He really knows how to put on an act.

SEEING RED

Many animals use bright colors to warn other animals that they are poisonous or taste bad. Would you pick up one of these poison dart frogs? Or would you heed their warning?

CHATTY COLORS

While the sailfish looks similar to the swordfish, this fish has a larger dorsal fin. Sailfish hunt in schools and change the colors of their scales to communicate with each other. The color changes also confuse their prey.

SO, IS IT LANGUAGE?

We have seen that animals can communicate in a number of ways. Can we call their noises language? What about an animal, such as a parrot, which has been trained to speak? Can we say that parrot is actually speaking a language?

WHAT DO YOU KNOW, KOKO?

Koko is a gorilla that was born at the San Francisco Zoo. She's famous all over the world because she has been taught to use sign language by her caregiver. Koko certainly knows a great many hand signals, but critics say she does not really understand, and is only copying what she's been shown. According to them, she isn't able to communicate because she does not send signals of her own.

WHAT DO YOU THINK?

There's no question that Koko's a very clever animal, and does far more than other gorillas, but we cannot say that she talks. We have learned a great deal from her, though, about how language develops.

WORD PLAY

You can have so much fun playing with words. Have you ever tried juggling the letters of your name around to see what other words you can make? Here are some examples using *Catherine: at, in, he, cat, rat, hat, eat, tea, her, are, car, care, near, neat, heat, then, heart, reach, there.* Can you find more?

WHO'S YOUR PAL?

Alert! Big word coming up: *palindrome.* Not really such a mouthful though, is it? A palindrome is a word, a group of words, or a number that is the same when read backward or forward. Some simple examples are *mom, pop, Anna, noon, kayak, radar,* and *madam.* Palindromes can be whole sentences, like: Madam, I'm Adam. Whoever thought of that one first must have really loved words, don't you think?

PUZZLING

A *riddle* is a puzzle of some sort. Word riddles are often in the form of a question. Try this one. Find the answer at the bottom of the page, upside down.

I'm in cookie
But not in cake
I'm in ocean
But not in lake
I am a letter
Not found in sweater

What am I?

CHANGING PLACES

We used the letters in *Catherine* to make up new words, some short and some long. New words made with all of the letters in a given word are called *anagrams.* If we use *cat,* as an example, we can make the word *act.* Get the idea? Here are some more.

pat – tap
ink – kin
pea – ape
war – raw
read – dear
race – care
fires – fries

Remember we talked about Otzi, the Iceman, and his ancient tattoos? *Iceman* is an anagram of *cinema.*

CAN GET CONFUSING

Big word alert! Have you heard of *homophones*? These are words that sound exactly the same, but have different spellings and different meanings. Consider this: The maid made the bed. Or this: They knew that I'm new here. Or this: The child threw the ball through the window. How many more can you find?

What about cross words and crosswords? How would you explain the difference?

Are you a wordsmith? Perhaps you are, but if you're not sure, a dictionary will tell you.

Answer: The fifteenth letter of the alphabet

INDEX

ACKNOWLEDGMENTS

My thanks are due to Charles Nurnberg, who believed in the concept of this book and helped bring it to life; Emily Bornoff, who illustrated it; and Melissa Gerber, who designed the layout and cover; my editor, Dawn Cusick, whose forbearance is greatly appreciated; and to my husband and family.

GLOSSARY

Bilingual: Someone who speaks two languages
Bioluminescence: Light produced by a living organism
Cuneiform: An ancient form of writing
Echolocation: Sound waves and echoes used to navigate
Esperanto: An invented language that's very simple to use
Hieroglyphics: A picture writing system used by ancient Egyptians
Linguist: A scholar who studies speech; a person who speaks several languages
Migrate: To move from one area to another
Pheromone: A substance given off by animals that affects behavior
Polyglot: Someone who speaks two or more languages
Scarification: Scars deliberately made on the body
Subtitles: Words written across the bottom of a movie or TV screen
Trademark: Symbols or words belonging to a company

ABOUT THE RESEARCH FOR THIS BOOK . . .

The following authors and sources provided valuable information:
Nathan Aaseng, Margaret Atwood, Raymond Bial, Laurel J. Brinton, E. A. Wallis Budge, Robert J. Conley, James M. Deem, Nell K. Duke, Charles D. Fennig, Julie Russ Harris, Edward Lear, Nonie K. Lesaux, Paul M. Lewis, Oxford Dictionaries, Gary F. Simons, and Webster's New World College Dictionaries